Water flows humbly to the lowest level.
Nothing is weaker than water,
Yet for overcoming what is hard and strong,
Nothing surpasses it.

~Lao Tzu

What he says.

~Tu Fu

Laughing Buddha Series

Tu Fu Comes to America

A Story in Poems

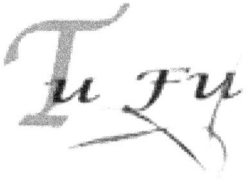

Translated by Larry Smith

Laughing Buddha Series
Bottom Dog Press
Huron, Ohio

© 2018 Larry Smith
& Bottom Dog Press
First edition by March Street Press (2010)
Second Expanded Edition

Some of these poems have appeared elsewhere:
"Tu Fu Enters the Cleveland Public Library"
in *13 Miles from Cleveland*.
"Tu Fu Talks to Barack Obama" and "Tu Fu Comes to Washington D.C."
in *The November 3rd Club*.

Contents:

Tu Fu Comes to America—7

Tu Fu Makes His Way South—9

Tu Fu Moves Up North—11

Tu Fu Passes the Winter in Ohio—14

Tu Fu Writes to His Wife—16

Tu Fu Is Given Notice—18

Tu Fu Works for AmeriTemp—20

Tu Fu Comes to Washington—23

Tu Fu Writes to Barack Obama—24

Tu Fu Counts His Blessings—26

Tu Fu Hears from Home—28

Tu Fu Writes an Old Friend—31

Tu Fu Enters the Arcade in Winter—32

Tu Fu Enters the Cleveland Public Library—36

Tu Fu Rides the RTA Bus—39

Tu Fu Buries Their Dog—40

Tu Fu at Work: Tanka—42

Tu Fu Follows the Cuyahoga—43

Tu Fu Visits the Diner on Lee Road—45

Tu Fu Is Interrupted—47

Tu Fu and Son Rake Leaves in the Suburbs—49

Tu Fu Listens for a Knocking—51

Tu Fu and Mei Liu Have a Sick Child—52

Tu Fu and Family Travel South—54

Tu Fu Surrenders—57

Author photo and biographic sketch—59

Dedication

To all friends of social justice, tolerance, and charcter.

Tu Fu Comes to America

1.
Jobless for two years now, I go out,
leave my sleeping wife and children
to walk the old road
before the cries of birds.

The path to a career cut off,
I must make myself another, and so
I ship for America on a dark freighter
crowded with bodies and voices.
These long nights we rock in nets
hanging from blank walls.
Only the smell of Taipei air
is stronger than this. On days
I thank each crack of light, and
begin to write in this little book.

Months ago brother Lang
had written of the good life in Canada,
and so, I've closed my eyes to enter
this mystery of another place.
One foot in China another in America,
my family there and our future here.

2.
Lang stands on the dock
where again we open our hearts and eyes
bowing to our family love.
We walk at dusk past maple trees
down the quiet streets of Quebec
to his room above the grocery shop
where he works. His wife Su Ying
and two sons make a humble home here.

We talk all night drinking tea,
yet in the morning light I know
that I must move on. And so
after three nights, a friend drives us
south for hours, where I say farewell again
and follow a pathway through trees.
Across the border I say a blessing
and pray my way south under moonlight.

Tu Fu Makes His Way South

With a sack and walking stick now
I tread the roads of West Virginia
back from noisy river towns,
down private hollows, up rocky hills
where farms nest and I can be
safe from questions.

Once an hour, a pick-up may pass,
staring at my foreign face.
Here time isn't measured so.
People sit out on porches
call to neighbors to come sit.
And so, I approach and bow,
then ask for a drink of water.
In my face they read a story
eyes meeting across porch steps.
"Come on up, outta the sun,"
they say and open their palms,
so that I sit on chair or stoop
cool shade across my lap.

Dogs run about the fenceless yard,
spring water in a clear glass jar.
I've traded hope for acceptance here,

find myself among new friends
in a land I was meant to know.
In soft sounds of late afternoon
they wait for me to speak.

Tu Fu Moves Up North

After weeks of doing odd jobs
and sleeping in neighbors' barns,
a friend from the home village writes Lang
of a job up north in Cleveland.
Pang works at a restaurant there
having moved from waiter to cook
to run The Golden Dragon.
Whispered over the phone, he says
 "Move north. Be my righthand cook."

No work here in West Virginia,
though the mountain and people
remind me so much of home.
Yet my need to bring family over presses,
and so up I go, bussing from Wheeling
through rugged foothills along the river,
one mill town after another,
then onto highways over plains.
I sleep, I write, I sleep, and then:
great lake spread out to the sky,
gulls circling over fishermen,
We've arrived at Ohio's north shore.
Tall buildings span the horizon,
then to the left and the right,

as the bus enters the station.
Outside seated on the pavement
two downcast men hold out cups
asking without any words.
I share my dollar with each.
Begging here in America
is seen through pity and shame.
The ways of Buddha are something
we must carry on inside.

With all my things on my back,
I make my way down the Avenue
then onto East 12th Street.
Busses and cars pass me, as I lean forward
breathe into my pain and smile.
A glass building rises before me,
its lights a beacon: The Galleria.
Inside such beauty and richness,
a moving stairway, flowers, music.
A security guard eyes me,
as I stroll past into the Food Court.
There among others: The Golden Dragon.
My friend's wife taps his shoulder,
and he turns to my open face
We share a bow through tears.
His smile rewards my travels.

After tea and rice and talk,
we begin my training at the hot table:
learning the dishes by heart,
memorizing the English words.
"This is not as we like it,"
he tells me, "but we must remember,
we feed the Americans now."
I work the rest of the day
beside Pang and his wife Li Mei
deep food smell entering my clothes.
At night we clean and put away,
then I follow them home
where I spread my mat on their floor
and sleep the night like a cat.

I wake with his two children
climbing over me. Their sweet faces
and gentle play tugs at my heart,
my own loved ones an ocean
and perhaps a year away.
I will work hard, save everything,
move in with the dishwasher,
cook my way to them someday soon.

Tu Fu Passes the Winter in Ohio

Days and weeks and months.
Slow melting snow
along the wide streets
washed away.
    *   *   *

With pen and ink
I touch my wife's face,
paper as smooth
as her skin.
    *   *   *

Black dog in the street
red car run up over curb.
Kneeling in wet snow
to water and blood.
    *   *   *

Wild geese call out
arrow through gray sky,
cold wind across my face
remembering.
    *   *   *

Past the catholic schoolyard
young girls in dark blue coats
spread their arms like wings
glide over fresh snow.

* * *

The wind at my window
snow swirling on the ground
beneath a street lamp.
Why sleep this night?

* * *

Old woman orders rice bowl,
the face of a chicken.
I dish some vegetables into a cup
her trembling hands.

* * *

My books gather in a corner
as old friends now.
Drinking hot tea
I write the night away.

* * *

I walk with my dog
over frost covered weeds
pull my coat against wind.
Lao-Tzu's new moon rising.

Tu Fu Writes to His Wife

When my father left me his job
working at the water plant,
I passed it on to my brother
who already had two children.
Besides, I was leading a bachelor life,
working and roaming when I would
like the wild geese, they say.
But then, at forty I saw—
I had only the worn clothes on my back,
some memories of places and friends,
all the books I had read
like empty bottles of wine.
Though I had done a few deeds of kindness,
I was neither scholar nor monk.
The few women I had met were in bars
or the good wives of friends.
And when they tried to fix me up
I would turn tail and run
like the pheasant. But then
in your father's field at dusk
I met, my love, you, and my days
of running came to an end. Your hair
was tied up in a red ribbon, your eyes
glowed in the firelight as you carried

bundles of wheat on your smooth shoulders.
When I offered to help, you touched my arm
and smiled under the full moon. "Ask father,"
you said and turned, and so the courting began
that August and September. I slept
in the loft of your barn, the cows and goats
making their soft music below. But I
watched you every day, working beside you,
till our bodies moved as one.

Your father never asked of my past.
Was it you who closed that door
to open another in my life?
Our children grow now, like the
flowers in your hair.

Tu Fu Is Given Notice

I tread to work this day—
the same shops and windows
the same morning rain.

Pang stands at the kitchen door
his arms at his side.
No lights are on inside.
We bow, and his face speaks.
"Bad news, my friend," he says,
as we sit in the darkened room.
"We are closed," he sighs,
"for good, I'm afraid."
His wife wipes a cloth
across the cold steam table.
His palm rises toward the ceiling.
"It's been sold to a pizza chain."

Silence fills the room and my heart.
I have sent all my monies
for my wife to book passage,
saving only for rent and rice.
This knife thrust into my chest—
who has delivered it?
Pain and anger are wed.

I've found them anew.
Pang rises, says, "Go home, Tu,"
his suffering face brother to my own.

Soaked, at last I pause
in the doorway of a shoe store,
watch gray pigeons circling about,
searching for food in the rain.
A drowning man does not need water
yet it comes washing over all,
reflecting what light remains.
I breathe our shared fear and pain,
hold it, taste it, release to soft light.

Tu Fu Works for AmeriTemp

It's a long walk down Murray Hill
treading over the leafy sidewalk
through Little Italy into the city.
No lights are on at five a.m.
except at Corbo's Bakery
where the smell of bread baking
in ovens overwhelms me.

In the alleyway behind
in the dumpster by the wall
they set out yesterday's buns.
I fill my mouth and a bag
to take home later tonight,
cast a couple in the wet grass
for the legend of pigeons.

I must be at AmeriTemp by six
yet it's two miles away.
On Euclid, I see Ted and Joe
walking down the other side.
We all find somewhere to sleep.

I catch up with them at the light
near the great concert hall,

gray stone and mirrored windows
looking out on us as we pass.
Joe reaches out to me,
and I hand him the best bun.
Ted's too proud to eat on the street
though Americans do it everywhere.
We walk on in silence, cross over
at the Clinic to Carnegie—
three men hungry for jobs.

At the Mission we wave to friends.
I lived there months when I arrived
knew them all by their names.
My wife and children back in China,
I worked and saved as in Hunan Province
until we brought them over, smuggled
across the border from Canada.
I could live without money, but not their faces.

We head down Prospect Street.
Inside the Temp building is a mirror:
"Would you hire this man?"

No one knows where we'll be
or if we'll work at all today.
Need and luck dictate our fate.

If picked, we grab our gloves
and board the vans. We pay
for the ride and only hope
they'll be there to bring us home.

It's mostly clean-up work
public buildings and stadiums
or factory jobs where grinders
and cutters can cost you a finger.
The harder the work, the less the pay.
I've learned, and the agency keeps half.
What can we do? We are
the working poor. I sit on the bench,
dream of walking in the door in time
to tuck the children into their beds.

Tu Fu Comes to Washington

A new leader has been called out
by those enslaved by the old—
a tyrant blind to his own heart.

My wife and children have moved
into the shelter in Cleveland,
and so I've hitched to the Capitol,
walking half the way.

Many sleep dreamless in the streets here
jobless and hungry for hope,
all of us conscripted to the banks or government.
A heavy snow lies about avenues,
a cold wind blows through the parks.

I rise from cardboard, stand in door fronts,
imagine the faces of my wife and children
standing in line for oatmeal and bread.

No wonder we gather at shop windows
to watch news of a leader risen among us.
His face smiles with kindness, and yet
in the sadness about his eyes
lies our real hope.

Tu Fu Writes to Barack Obama

This morning I woke beside the road
and walked seven miles
across your state of Virginia,
then took the railway into town—
so many faces, so many voices,
different tongues from different lands.

On the train I sat and watched:
they all looked forward to this city,
many mute, all with some need
etched into their face.

One woman complained of her cancer,
said she'd come to stand outside your window
here with me. An old man near the station
begged for my change.

I know your days are busy;
this country's needed leaders for years now.

Send the Congress into the streets
to know the thirst and hunger,
the Senate to the battlefields
where lives are spent like loose change.

Don't give up until they know
the waste of waiting for reform.

If you could see the young girl's face
riding beside me, pregnant
with the hope of seeing you.

Tu Fu Counts His Blessings

Sparrows gather in the back yard
and sit on the fence posts
without any necks. Last summer
we fed them sunflower seeds.
Now our own stores are so diminished
I sneak the food of birds.
Jobless for almost a year now
I sold our beloved dog to hunters
to pay a little rent. My wife
cleans the houses of others, yet
neglects our own. We have so little hope.
My boy wears my old shoes
stuffed with newspaper
to school with his friends.
None of them better than the rest.
The poems I write at night
do nothing to heat this house.
Our bodies are so cold they
shake as trains go rattling by.

The sink will not drain, and
I've already sold all my tools.
We can't afford a plumber
so I go walking down the street

asking the help of others. No soap.
At noon I slip into a tavern
and sit inside the dark—
without a dime to my name.
My father's curse when I left the farm
to work in the mills: "You'll starve!"
he called as I drove away.
The chickens up in the trees.
A friend at the bar buys me a beer,
and I repay him with a smile that
costs me a sharp pain in the gut—
A father's sins of failing those who love him
can't just be washed away.

Out in the street I meet my wife
and her silence screams into my face.
Together we walk back to our little place
where our young daughter Li Mei wraps
her thin arms around my legs.

Tu Fu Hears from Home

I received a letter from my sister
back in the Hunan home province.
I still see her as a child
though I know she's now a mother.
She used to sit on the ground
put small stones into her mouth.
Brother and I would turn away
from this girl with a dirty face,
her blue eyes smiling up at us.

She writes in a delicate hand
on this onion skin paper
to tell us how things have changed.
New industry everywhere
where once were rice fields.
"Where have the birds gone?" she asks.
"It's hard to find anything green
except for our bonsai plants.
People tuck tine gardens
in the strip between the highway."

Her family is well she says
"Everyone works all the time.
Though the wages are low,

and the bosses rule like warlords."
They hope to see their son Li
go to college in America.
"Could you please help?" she asks,
"a sister's humble request."
How can I tell her how poor we are,
that my own children must beg
outside the railway station.

We have come so far
to be where we are. Poverty
a dark hawk at our footsteps.
My skills at writing poems
pay even less over here.
My children's faces stare up
from the papers I write upon,
and so my hands grow calloused
from shovels and brooms.
Today my children and I
went up and down neighborhoods
asking if we could rake their leaves.
This life moves slowly like the stars
or the yellow river toward the sea.

Mei Mei closes her letter
remembering other times,

"How the tree in the yard
beside our little house
would fill with white blossoms,
petals to be blown in the wind."

Tu Fu Writes an Old Friend

Nothing has changed, my friend.
The snows lay heavy on the ground,
each layer a day that's passed.
We don't go out for long,
lake wind gets under our clothes.

I feed the birds our leftover millet.
They huddle and wait.
Only we question the weather.

When I was young I wrote my poems
in ink on fine papers, learning calligraphy
to turn them into art. Now I
write on the backs of envelopes
forgetting them for days at a time.

I'll copy this onto a postcard for you,
place it into the hands of the postman.
Next month I'll hitch a ride to your place
and we'll talk and drink under a full moon.
I set down my pen and look out the window;
first light comes on through the pines.

Tu Fu Enters the Arcade in Winter

Again, no work at Ameritemp,
too cold for outside work,
so I tramp down Euclid
in the early morning light.
Snow swirls around my feet
and into pockets of doorways.
My coat can't stop the wind
from sending chills through me,
and so I stop before the Arcade:
huge dark stones, new glass doors,
lights inside inviting me.
The doorman eyeing me as I
follow a pretty shop girl
dressed in black jacket and skirt
through the revolving doors.

Warmth kisses my face and hands.
My eyes water as they stare
into a flower shop window—
Spring in Winter in Ohio.
I keep moving as though a worker
past the eyes of the hotel clerk.
The Hyatt-Regency
has taken over the Arcade

turning convenience into luxury.
Shining brass rails are everywhere,
gold gargoyles guard the towers.
My eyes lift skyward
to the glass cathedral ceiling
that stops my breath…
I must bring Mei and the children here.
Man has made this, I think,
a palace for the people
more grand than the Imperial Palace.

A guard walks toward me
so I duck down the marble stairway
toward the basement shops
where I might find food or work.
The warm smell of baking
draws me to a Chinese restaurant.
I tap on the window
and a man turns to face me.
Quick he crosses his hands
to say they are closed. I smile
and make the dish washing gesture.
He does not shun me but comes out
"Please," I say, head down,
"Could you use the help today?"
He looks at me hard,

checks my hands and says quick,
"You work for the minimum—
wash pots and pans—Okay?"
I nod and follow him in
as the security guard turns away.
We cross through the dark table area
and enter the push doors of a bright kitchen.
Two men and a woman grow silent
as they rush about stewing sauces;
one cuts carrots, cabbage, and celery.

I am taken to the back
where an old man greets me.
"Ah, my helper for the day,"
he smiles and shakes my hand
with his own, warm and red
from running the dishwasher.
"My name is Tu," I say,
taking the apron. "Mine's Ed,
and you've got the pots today,"
and he points to a crusty stack
on and under the sink.
"Sam up and quit last night.
You might have yourself a job—
if you can take the abuse."
Pots and pans never looked so good.

By nine-thirty before first customers,
Sam and I take our coffee break
at the tables out near the stairs.
He hands me a stack of old cookies,
"This building," I say, "is magnificent."
And he, "The Crystal Palace they call it,
built a hundred years ago by
Cleveland's millionaires: Hanna,
Harkness and Rockefeller."
I gaze up again at the tiered balconies.
"All that's the Hyatt now," he says.
"Can't enter without a key.
Rooms is near $200 a night."
I lower my eyes to our level.
"Used to be book and cigar stores,
bakeries, coin shops, hot dog stand
out in the tower at Superior.
Now it's all boutique and upscale.
Gone back to the rich and famous."
I hear all of his lament
but can't take in his misery now,
too happy to find work for these hands.

Tu Fu Enters the Cleveland Public Library

They didn't need me today,
said Old Ed could handle things—
few customers, but I know too
it's to keep me from full-time
and collecting benefits.
Yet they wait till I show up,
so I stand here in early light
waiting for Bus 10 to take me home.
An old woman standing near
looks over at me and speaks,
"I clean for people out in Shaker.
How about you?" She's dressed warm
in what they call a Pea coat,
her brass buttons shining in street light.
"I do dishes at Ming's, but
today they don't need me," I shrug;
she nods, knowing the way it is.
I stare out across Superior.
Lights come on in the long gray building.
"That's our library," she says,
and her words hang in the air
as a gush of traffic passes.

I stare at the grand doors,

then find myself crossing,
climbing the broad stone steps.
I enter the quiet space
passing under the watchful eyes
of a blue uniformed guard
and into a huge dome,
arches over every door and window.
I carry nothing to check,
only my pocket notebook
where I scribble my poems.
A woman in blue suit smiles.
"You're our first customer today,"
she says. "How may I direct you?"
And I think to say: "Literature—Chinese."
"That would be our second floor,
up that stairway." I bow slightly
and walk to the marbled steps,
a huge painting spread before me.
In such space and richness
I feel both large and small.
I climb, then enter an archway
to a room as wide as a field.
Lost among shelves of books,
always my friends and guides,
I am stranger again in a city of words.
I pass the dim blue light

of computer screens, finding my way
down the marked streets of bookshelves
till I come to "PJ"—my poetry home place.
My hand skims the textured wall
of books of varied colors.
I smell the glue of aged pages.
and would choose them all—
devour them there among the stacks.
The world dissolves outside the windows.
On a stool I feed for hours
take down old Lao Tzu:
as darkness lightens,
    murky comes clear,
and stillness moves.

At noon I take out my pen.

Tu Fu Rides the RTA Bus

We've paid our bills again this month,
and the children are all in schools.
While drinking tea on Sunday
sitting on the back-porch steps
my wife said she wants to learn English,
not with friends but at night school.
I don't know all that this means.
The new ways come on in waves
covering us, shaking our legs in sand
but then subside, leaving us standing.
Does Mei Liu find herself anew?
And who am I in this moment?

Riding this bus, I close my eyes
feel all of us moving together,
not just these faces, but all—
the tires thump, the brakes gush
and the door opens—some get off,
some get on—a sea of faces.
I hold the bar, brace myself
lean forward as we push onward.
In the shopping bag, my work clothes,
on my back, the white shirt Mei has ironed.
No yesterday or tomorrow, only now.

Tu Fu Buries Their Dog

Before our evening meal, he broke loose
ran out into the street at dusk
as a delivery truck passed by.
We heard the yelp before the brakes.
Jong ran to the window and cried out:
"They've killed our dog," as if attacked
as we were in the villages back home
where things were just taken or killed.

Here dogs are brought into the home,
given names like family members.
"Tao" was what we called him,
and he slept on the floor by our bed.
We walked with him down streets,
along the lake and into the woods.
He liked to ramble about, coming back
at times smelling of fish.

I brought the shovel out and
scooped him into a cardboard box.
In China we burn the bodies.
Here private fires are forbidden.

And so we've taken Tao back

into the woods where he roamed.
The children help to dig, then
gather stones, cover it all
with fresh fallen leaves.

I look out to the East and the West
my feet planted now in Ohio.

Tu Fu at Work: Tanka

Watching on millyard bench as
lace shadows of fire escape steps
inch down the brick wall.
I breathe in the hot air
await the sun's release.

* * *

Young red-haired woman
wearing tin mill blue carries her
lunch pail next her breasts.
Beyond those calls of track crew,
she tucks her children into bed.

* * *

Pushing the wheelbarrow
uphill with bags of lime
waiting for Joe's silent nod.
Humble machine, countryless,
I follow your simple grace.

* * *

With others at the time clock
I stand with card in hand
awaiting the next click.
The old guy I worked with today
lives just across the street.

Tu Fu Follows the Cuyahoga

No work today, and so I walk
down Euclid past the Public Square
where the traffic swells at the light.
At Terminal Tower, Ted stands
outside the revolving doors
selling *Grapevines* to shoppers.
But I walk on toward the river,
follow a path under Superior Bridge
great cement legs and arms
spanning the Cuyahoga.

I jump the tracks, head down
to a weedy spot along the edge.
The river streams out into the lake,
quiet amidst the city's roar.
I stand at the turn where bridges
lift and swing and jackknife
into gray morning sky, and I
am back on the Yellow River
holding a bamboo fishing pole
while the sun rises slowly
over rows of huts. Two worlds
unite in me. I stare into water
know again the forever of all

that departs and arrives. My eyes follow a great V of wild geese winging south along the river.

Tu Fu Visits the Diner on Lee Road

    (Cleveland Heights 2010)

We've moved to a small apartment
near the Seven Eleven on Lee Road.
My wife and me, and three kids,
our dog and two cats
(We don't eat them, you know,
though Americans joke that we do.)

Our dog Tao II isn't happy
since we no longer have a yard.
So I walk him a lot
down Lee Road to the diner,
a new one dressed like the old,
though it's all new to me.

I tie Tao to a fence post
and sit where I can watch him.
The chrome and mirrors inside
hurt my eyes each time I enter,
but I'll tell you the truth,
I go there for Rochelle
who waitresses there most days.
Her red hair is kept up
well away from the food,

but I'd love to see it down
to frame her pretty blue eyes.
Her beauty troubles me;
her youth tortures me.

When she takes my order
I follow her words to her lips.
Her breasts rise and fall with her breath.
In truth I want to order her.
She always gives me scraps for Tao.

Though I know she has two kids
and I do love my wife Mei Liu,
I collect bottles and aluminum cans
for change to buy coffee and toast.
Though she calls me 'honey," I know
I share that with all her customers.
Yet today I catch her eyes
looking into mine, and when
she touches my hand with the bill,
I understand for the first time
my father's taking a concubine.

When I untie Tao, I know at last
I must bid farewell to Rochelle and
to this my breakfast place.

Tu Fu Is Interrupted

I set out to write a poem
of the sudden turning of leaves
while others sleep through the dawn.
As my words appear on paper
a loud knocking comes to our door.
A tall man in gray overalls
hands me a yellow sheet
then stares into my eyes, says
he's come to shut off our water.
He turns to go down the stairs
into the apartment's cold basement.
His heavy footsteps obtrude
on my uneven breathing.

I stare down at his paper
in my blank and useless hand.
Only my eyes tell me
he has the wrong name and number.
In my robe I rush after him
my hair still wild from dreams.
At the bottom of the steps
he turns on me quick, black
flashlight held high in defense.
I bow my head, extend the sheet—

"Sir," I offer, "the name and number
are not ours." I wait in darkness
for his eyes to register.

He speaks aloud the name
of our old neighbor "Chang Li,"
and a sharp pang enters my chest.
My only thoughts to save us
clamped shut my mind and heart.
"Sorry," he says and turns
to climb the steps again.
"Wait," I speak. "How much?"
In the dim light of cold walls
he shrugs his shoulders,
"Not up to me…And besides
it's too late." I stand there,
mute and knowing that
my poem today will be traded
for hours of standing in line.

Tu Fu and Son Rake Leaves in the Suburbs

My eldest son Liu and I
with rakes on our shoulders
walk a mile past lighted shops
and restaurants on Coventry
into the rich neighborhoods
of Shaker Heights, where houses
rise from lawns like palaces.
It is Sunday in America
and the leaves have blown down
after two days of wind and rain.

We go up to the side doors
and knock and wait with smiles
painted across our faces.
When someone comes, they see at once
and only ask, "How much?"
I offer, "What you think is right,"
and if it brings a smile,
we know the job is ours.

Liu speaks little, works hard,
his eyes set on each task.
At ten he knows already
to answer need with action.

His rake extends his young arms
shooting out and drawing in
like a wave upon lake sand.
We gather into piles
bright leaves, wet and dry,
browns and reds and yellow.
Together we stuff them into bags.

In the bush near the bird feeder
Liu finds a dead bird—
the work of some neighbor's cat.
He sets its broken body
on the cold cement steps,
takes a wooden stake and digs
between the roots of the oak.
He buries it in the wet ground
while above our heads a wing
of wild geese call out.

Tu Fu Listens for a Knocking

Last night when I got home
I watched a white-green van
pull away from our little street.
Everyone knows the border patrol.
They watch our neighborhood
like guard dogs at the wrecking yard.
If we give them cause,
they'll be knocking at our door.
And so we stay inside, quiet,
like the sheep we must become.

Their dark uniforms fill my dreams,
yet I do not hate them. They saved
Juan's daughter from two men
in a black van as she walked home
from dancing class at school.
All parents know that fear.
Human trafficking—nothing new to us,
but even a Buddhist knows a sin
when it's in your neighborhood,
when it's in your face. And so
we live with their narrow watching
and pray their hearts stay open.

Tu Fu and Mei Liu Have a Sick Child

Our daughter Rose is sick with something
we can't recognize, and so
we have brought her here
to the Free Clinic on Euclid.
We sit on plastic chairs and wait
while a doctor examines our Rose.
Our neighbor Paul drove us here at dawn,
after two hospitals turned us away.
Mei and I had spent the night
pressing damp cloths to her small body
trying to bring the fever down.
Rose's eyes would stare out at us
then drift away with the pain.

Wordless we avoided each other's looks
remembering the death of baby Chang Li;
his blue eyes floated then shut forever
closing our hearts then to our life.
The pain was more than we could bear
and so we ate the bitter rice and
ignored the suffering of others.
One evening I stumbled home
to find Mei gone and the children alone.
It began raining and I heard a knock;

a soldier had puller her from the river.
When she awoke, we held each other
and rocked for hours. Then
I rose to make cabbage soup,
stroking each child on the cheek

So now we breathe through
our heart's retreat, tasting our fears,
ready to trade our lives on promise,
yet keeping our eyes open
to the other faces in this room—
The old woman alone at the window,
the tired mother cradling her sick child.
Mei moves over to sit with them.
I listen to the story of a
young man with wild hair and eyes.
We pass the time together
till the nurse comes over to take us back
where standing over our Rose,
a young doctor turns.

Tu Fu and Family Travel South

An old friend asks us to visit,
and so we pack some things
walk down Chester Avenue
to board the Greyhound bus.
So many faces at the station,
so many gather on our bus.
My wife and I sit together,
the children close behind.
We listen to the chatter of birds,
stare out the big windows
as the station moves behind us
and we forwards into afternoon.

As we ride along Ohio fields
we talk softly then drift into sleep.

Our friend from Hunan Province
lives along the River Ohio
in a valley laced with trees,
the town laid out like a garden
around dark and heavy industry,
smoke stacks rising to the sky.
The children press faces and words
to the window glass. My wife

places her hand in mine.

The bus pulls up to a diner
and stops—a gush of air
as the door rushes open.
"East Liverpool," he announces,
and we gather our back packs
depart the bus steps like school children.
The air tastes of smoke and wind,
yet a quiet lies over this town.

We have arrived early and so
wait an hour on the diner steps,
till Chang-Li pulls up in his old car.
Standing together in twilight
he bows then extends his hand
as they do in America, says,
"I'm so happy you have come....
I had to leave my wife at home
so we all could fit in my car."
We all smile and bow again.
Good friends are more than gold
when we are far from home.

He drives past old stone ovens
where bricks once were pressed and baked—

monuments to a lost industry.
Across the bridge a steel mill
sleeps along the river. "Shut down,"
Chang says and lifts his head,
"We're all learning to survive."
"Always," I say into his eyes.
Silence fills the car as we drive.

We arrive in darkness
yet his house if full of light.
Warm Chinese faces reflect our own
as we sit at the kitchen table
drinking tea and remembering.
Old stories dissolve into new,
as our families sit together
sipping tea and going on.

Tu Fu Surrenders

Two years now I've lived
in America.
No further along
than when I arrived.
No further behind.
My children watch tv,
my wife talks on the phone.
We can't afford a car,
besides, we are illegals.

How to measure and why?

Today at the market
I watched a chicken
be hatcheted
without a sound.
And another
ran down the street
screaming at cars.
I sat on a curb
and whistled,
sunlight falling
on my face and arms.

Larry Smith, a native Midwesterner, is a graduate of Muskingum College and Kent State University (M.A. and Ph.D). He is the author of 9 books of poetry, 2 books of memoirs, 5 books of fiction, 2 literary biographies of authors Lawrence Ferlinghetti and Kenneth Patchen. Together with Mei Hui Huang he has translated two books from the Chinese poets: *What Hold Has this Mountain: Chinese Zen Poems* and *The Kanshi Poems of Taigu Ryokan*. With flutist Monte Page he produced the audio booklet *Songs of the Woodcutter: Zen Poems of Wang Wei & Taigu Ryokan*.

As a professor emeritus of English and humanities at Bowling Green State University's Firelands College he has taught writing and literature and served as director of the Firelands Writing Center, a cooperative of writers. As director of the literary publisher, Bottom Dog Press, Inc., he has edited over 60 books and carried into publication some 208 titles of poetry, fiction, and nonfiction. In addition, Smith is a consultant and reviewer for such publications as *New York Journal of Books*, Wayne State University Press, *American Book Review, Parabola, Small Press Review, Choice, The San Francisco Review of Books, The Columbus Dispatch, Ohioana Quarterly, Heartlands* and *Shambhala Sun Magazine*. His poetry has been featured on American Public Media's *Writer's Almanac* with Garrison Keillor. His second chapbook in the March Street Press series is *Each Moment All: Poems*, now published by Bottom Dog Press.

www.ingramcontent.com/pod-product-compliance
Lightning Source LLC
Chambersburg PA
CBHW021000090426
42736CB00010B/1402